THE EXCELLENCY OF CHRIST

The Excellency of Christ

BY

Jonathan Edwards, A.M.
Pastor of the Church in *Northampton,* Massachusetts

Minneapolis

Published by Curiosmith.
P. O. Box 390293, Minneapolis, Minnesota, 55439.
Internet: curiosmith.com.
E-mail: shopkeeper@curiosmith.com.

The Outline of the Contents was added to this edition by the publisher.

Previously published—Boston: Printed and Sold by S. Kneeland and T. Green, in Queen-street over against the Prison, 1738.

Supplementary content and cover design:
Copyright © 2012 Charles J. Doe.

ISBN 9781935626466

OUTLINE OF THE CONTENTS

Two distinct appellations here given to Christ. (PAGE 11.)
1. He is called the *Lion*. (PAGE 11.)
2. He is called a *Lamb*. (PAGE 12.)

First, Show wherein there is an admirable conjunction of diverse excellencies in Jesus Christ. (PAGE 13.)

I. There is a conjunction of such excellencies in Christ, as, in our manner of conceiving, are very diverse one from another. (PAGE 13.)
   1. There do meet in Jesus Christ infinite highness and infinite condescension.
   2. There meet in Jesus Christ, infinite *justice* and infinite *grace.*

II. There is in him a conjunction of such really diverse excellencies, as otherwise would have seemed to us utterly incompatible in the same subject. (PAGE 17.)
   1. In the person of Christ do meet together infinite *glory* and lowest *humility.*
   2. In the person of Christ do meet together infinite *majesty* and transcendent *meekness.*
   3. There meet in the person of Christ the deepest *reverence* towards God and *equality* with God.
   4. There are conjoined in the person of Christ infinite *worthiness* of good, and the greatest *patience* under sufferings of evil.
   5. In the person of Christ are conjoined an exceeding spirit of *obedience*, with supreme *dominion* over heaven and earth.
   6. In the person of Christ are conjoined absolute *sovereignty* and perfect *resignation.*
   7. In Christ do meet together *self-sufficiency*, and an entire *trust* and reliance on God.

(Continued on the next page.)

OUTLINE OF THE CONTENTS (Continued)

 III. Such diverse excellencies are exercised in him towards men that otherwise would have seemed impossible to be exercised towards the same object; as particularly these three, justice, mercy, and truth. (PAGE 25.)

Secondly, To show how this admirable conjunction of excellencies appears in Christ's *acts.* (PAGE 27.)

 I. It appears in what Christ did in taking on him our nature. (PAGE 27.)

 II. It appears in the acts and various passages of Christ's life. (PAGE 29.)

 III. It appears in his offering up himself a sacrifice for sinners in his last sufferings. (PAGE 33.)

  1. Then was Christ in the greatest degree of his humiliation, and yet by that, above all other things, his divine glory appears.

  2. He never in any act gave so great a manifestation of love to God, and yet never so manifested his love to those that were enemies to God, as in that act.

  3. Christ never so eminently appeared *for* divine justice, and yet never suffered so much *from* divine justice, as when he offered up himself a sacrifice for our sins.

  4. Christ's holiness never so illustriously shone forth as it did in his last sufferings; and yet he never was to such a degree treated as guilty.

  5. He never was so dealt with, as unworthy, as in his last sufferings; and yet it is chiefly on account of them that he is accounted worthy.

  6. Christ in his last sufferings suffered most extremely from those towards whom he was then manifesting his greatest act of love.

  7. It was in Christ's last sufferings, above all, that he was delivered up to the power of his enemies; and yet by these, above all, he obtained victory over his enemies.

 IV. It is still manifest in his acts, in his present state of exaltation in heaven. (PAGE 42.)

 V. It will be manifest in Christ's acts at the last judgment. (PAGE 44.)

(Continued on the next page.)

OUTLINE OF THE CONTENTS (Continued)

APPLICATION (PAGE 45.)
I. From this doctrine we may learn one reason why Christ is called by such a variety of names, and held forth under such a variety of representations, in Scripture. (PAGE 45.)
II. Let the consideration of this wonderful meeting of diverse excellencies in Christ induce you to accept of him, and close with him as your Saviour. (PAGE 47.)
   1. What are you afraid of, that you dare not venture your soul upon Christ? (PAGE 49.)
   2. What is there that you can desire should be in a Saviour, that is not in Christ? (PAGE 50.)
      (1.) How much Christ appears as the Lamb of God in his invitations to you to come to him and trust in him.
      (2.) If you do come to Christ, he will appear as a Lion, in his glorious power and dominion, to defend you.
III. Let what has been said be improved to induce you to love the Lord Jesus Christ, and choose him for your friend and portion. (PAGE 56.)
   1. Christ will give himself to you, with all those various excellencies that meet in him, to your full and everlasting enjoyment. (PAGE 61.)
   2. By your being united to Christ, you will have a more glorious union with and enjoyment of God the Father, than otherwise could be. (PAGE 65.)

THE EXCELLENCY OF CHRIST[1]

A SERMON BY

JONATHAN EDWARDS, A.M.

And one of the elders saith unto me, Weep not: behold, the Lion of the tribe of Juda, the Root of David, hath prevailed to open the book, and to loose the seven seals thereof. And I beheld, and, lo, in the midst of the throne, and of the four beasts, and in the midst of the elders, stood a Lamb as it had been slain.—REVELATION 5:5, 6.

THE visions and revelations the apostle John had of the future events of God's providence, are here introduced with a vision of the book of God's decrees, by which those events were foreordained. This is represented (verse 1.) as a book in the right hand of him who sat on the throne, "written within and on the back side, and sealed with seven seals." Books, in the form in which they were wont of old to be made, were broad leaves of parchment or paper, or something of that nature, joined together at one edge, and so rolled up together, and then sealed, or some way fastened together, to prevent their unfolding

---

[1] The Excellency of Christ; a sermon preached at Northampton, in New England, in the time of the wonderful work of grace there, [printed] in the year 1738.

and opening. Hence we read of the roll of a book, Jeremiah 36:2. It seems to have been such a book that John had a vision of here; and therefore it is said to be "written within and on the back side," *i.e.* on the inside pages, and also on one of the outside pages, *viz.* that which was rolled in, in rolling the book up together. And it is said to be "sealed with seven seals," to signify that what was written in it was perfectly hidden and secret; or that God's decrees of future events are sealed, and shut up from all possibility of being discovered by creatures, till God is pleased to make them known. We find that seven is often used in Scripture as the number of perfection, to signify the superlative or most perfect degree of any thing; which probably arose from this, that on the seventh day God beheld the works of creation finished, and rested and rejoiced in them, as being complete and perfect.

When John saw this book, he tells us, he "saw a strong angel proclaiming with a loud voice, Who is worthy to open the book, and to loose the seals thereof? And no man in heaven, nor in earth, neither under the earth, was able to open the book, neither to look thereon." And that he wept much, because "no man was found worthy to open and read the book, neither to look thereon." And then tells us how his tears were dried up, *viz.* that "one of the elders said unto him, Weep not; Behold the Lion of the tribe of Judah hath prevailed,"[2] etc. as in the

2 Revelation 5:2–5.

text. Though no man nor angel, nor any mere creature, was found either able to loose the seals, or worthy to be admitted to the privilege of reading the book; yet this was declared, for the comfort of this beloved disciple, that Christ was found both able and worthy. And we have an account in the succeeding chapters how he actually did it, opening the seals in order, first one, and then another, revealing what God had decreed should come to pass hereafter. And we have an account in this chapter, of his coming and taking the book out of the right hand of him that sat on the throne, and of the joyful praises that were sung to him in heaven and earth on that occasion.

Many things might be observed in the words of the text; but it is to my present purpose only to take notice of the two distinct appellations here given to Christ.

1. He is called the *Lion*. *Behold, the Lion of the tribe of Judah*. He seems to be called the Lion of the tribe of Judah, in allusion to what Jacob said in his blessing of the tribes on his death-bed; who, when he came to bless Judah, compares him to a lion, Genesis 49:9. "Judah is a lion's whelp; from the prey, my son, thou art gone up: he stooped down, he couched as a lion, and as an old lion; who shall rouse him up?" And also to the standard of the camp of Judah in the wilderness, on which was displayed a lion, according to the ancient tradition of the Jews. It is much on account of the valiant acts of David

that the tribe of Judah, of which David was, is in Jacob's prophetical blessing compared to a lion; but more especially with an eye to Jesus Christ, who also was of that tribe, and was descended of David, and is in our text called "the Root of David;" and therefore Christ is here called "the Lion of the tribe of Judah."

2. He is called a *Lamb*. John was told of a Lion that had prevailed to open the book, and probably expected to see a lion in his vision; but while he is expecting, behold a Lamb appears to open the book, an exceeding diverse kind of creature from a lion. A lion is a devourer, one that is wont to make terrible slaughter of others; and no creature more easily falls a prey to him than a lamb. And Christ is here represented not only as a Lamb, a creature very liable to be slain, but a "Lamb as it had been slain," that is, with the marks of its deadly wounds appearing on it.

That which I would observe from the words, for the subject of my present discourse, is this, *viz.*—

"There is an admirable conjunction of diverse excellencies in Jesus Christ."

The lion and the lamb, though very diverse kinds of creatures, yet have each their peculiar excellencies. The lion excels in strength, and in the majesty of his appearance and voice: the lamb excels in meekness and patience, besides the excellent nature of the creature as good for food, and yielding that which is fit for our clothing, and being suitable to be offered in sacrifice

to God. But we see that Christ is in the text compared to both; because the diverse excellencies of both wonderfully meet in him,—In handling this subject I would,
First, Show wherein there is an admirable conjunction of diverse excellencies in Christ.
Secondly, How this admirable conjunction of excellencies appear in Christ's acts.
And then make application.

First, I would show wherein there is an admirable conjunction of diverse excellencies in Jesus Christ. Which appears in three things:
I. There is a conjunction of such excellencies in Christ, as, in our manner of conceiving, are very diverse one from another.
II. There is in him a conjunction of such really diverse excellencies, as otherwise would have seemed to us utterly incompatible in the same subject.
III. Such diverse excellencies are exercised in him towards men that otherwise would have seemed impossible to be exercised towards the same object.

I. There is a conjunction of such excellencies in Christ, as, in our manner of conceiving, are very diverse one from another. Such are the various divine perfections and excellencies that Christ is possessed of. Christ is a divine person; and therefore has all the attributes of God. The difference between these is chiefly relative, and in our manner of conceiving them. And those which, in this sense, are most diverse, meet

in the person of Christ. I shall mention two instances.
1. There do meet in Jesus Christ infinite highness and infinite condescension. Christ, as he is God, is infinitely great and high above all. He is higher than the kings of the earth, for he is King of kings, and Lord of lords. He is higher than the heavens, and higher than the highest angels of heaven. So great is he, that all men, all kings and princes, are as worms of the dust before him; all nations are as the drop of the bucket, and the light dust of the balance; yea, and angels themselves are as nothing before him. He is so high, that he is infinitely above any need of us; above our reach, that we cannot be profitable to him; and above our conceptions, that we cannot comprehend him. Proverbs 30:4. "What is his name, and what is his Son's name, if thou canst tell?" Our understandings, if we stretch them never so far, cannot reach up to his divine glory. Job 11:8. "It is high as heaven, what canst thou do?" Christ is the Creator and great Possessor of heaven and earth. He is sovereign Lord of all. He rules over the whole universe, and doth whatsoever pleaseth him. His knowledge is without bound. His wisdom is perfect, and what none can circumvent. His power is infinite, and none can resist him. His riches are immense and inexhaustible. His majesty is infinitely awful.

And yet he is one of infinite condescension. None are so low or inferior, but Christ's condescension is sufficient to take a gracious notice of them. He condescends not only to the angels, humbling himself to behold the things that are done in heaven, but he also condescends to such poor creatures as men; and that not only so as to take notice of princes and great men, but of those that are of meanest rank and degree, "the poor of the world," James 2:5. Such as are commonly despised by their fellow-creatures, Christ does not despise. 1 Corinthians 1:28. "Base things of the world, and things that are despised, hath God chosen." Christ condescends to take notice of beggars, Luke 16:22, and people of the most despised nations. In Christ Jesus is neither "Barbarian, Scythian, bond nor free," Colossians 3:11. He that is thus high, condescends to take a gracious notice of little children, Matthew 19:14. "Suffer little children to come unto me." Yea, which is more, his condescension is sufficient to take a gracious notice of the most unworthy, sinful creatures, those that have no good deservings, and those that have infinite ill-deservings.

Yea, so great is his condescension, that it is not only sufficient to take some gracious notice of such as these, but sufficient for every thing that is an act of condescension. His condescension is great enough to become their friend; to become their companion, to unite their souls to him in spiritual marriage. It is enough to take their nature upon him, to become one of them, that he may be one with them. Yea, it is great enough to abase himself yet lower for them, even to expose himself to shame and spitting; yea, to yield up himself to an ignominious death for them. And what act of condescension can be conceived of greater? Yet such an act as this, has his condescension yielded to, for those that are so low and mean, despicable and unworthy!

Such a conjunction of infinite highness and low condescension, in the same person, is admirable. We see, by manifold instances, what a tendency a high station has in men, to make them to be of a quite contrary disposition. If one worm be a little exalted above another, by having more dust, or a bigger dunghill, how much does he make of himself! What a distance does he keep from those that are below him! And a little condescension is what he expects should be made much of, and greatly acknowledged. Christ condescends to wash our feet; but how would great men, (or rather the bigger worms,) account themselves debased by acts of far less condescension!

2. There meet in Jesus Christ, infinite *justice* and infinite *grace*. As Christ is a divine person, he is infinitely holy and just; hating sin, and disposed to execute condign punishment for sin. He is the Judge of the world, and the infinitely just Judge of it, and will not at all acquit the wicked, or by any means clear the guilty.

And yet he is infinitely gracious and merciful. Though his justice be so strict with respect to all sin, and every breach of the law, yet he has grace sufficient for every sinner, and even the chief of sinners. And it is not only sufficient for the most unworthy to show them mercy, and bestow some good upon them, but to bestow the greatest good; yea, it is sufficient to bestow all good upon them, and to do all things for them. There is no benefit or blessing that they can receive, so great but the grace of Christ is sufficient to bestow it on the greatest sinner that ever lived. And not only so, but so great is his grace, that nothing is too much as the means of this good. It is sufficient not only to do great things, but also to suffer in order to it; and not only to suffer, but to suffer most extremely even unto death, the most terrible of natural evils; and not only death, but the most ignominious and tormenting, and every way the most terrible that men could inflict; yea, and greater sufferings than men could inflict, who could only torment the body. He had sufferings in his soul, that were the more immediate fruits of the wrath of God against the sins of those he undertakes for.

II. There do meet in the person of Christ such really diverse excellencies, which otherwise would have been thought utterly incompatible in the same subject; such as are conjoined in no other person whatever, either divine, human, or angelical; and such as neither men nor angels would ever have imagined could have met together in the same person, had it not been seen in the person of Christ. I would give some instances.

1. In the person of Christ do meet together infinite *glory* and lowest *humility*. Infinite glory, and the virtue of humility, meet in no other person but Christ. They meet in no created person; for no created person has infinite glory; and they meet in no other divine person but Christ. For though the divine nature be infinitely abhorrent to pride, yet humility is not properly predicable of God the Father, and the Holy Ghost, that exists only in the divine nature; because it is proper excellency only of a created nature; for it consists radically in a sense of a comparative lowness and littleness before God, or the great distance between God and the subject of this virtue; but it would be a contradiction to suppose any such thing in God.

But in Jesus Christ, who is both God and man, those two diverse excellencies are sweetly united. He is a person infinitely exalted in glory and dignity. Philippians 2:6. "Being in the form of God, he thought it not robbery to be equal with God." There is equal honour due to him with the Father. John 5:23—"That all men should honour the Son, even as they honour the Father." God himself says to him, "Thy throne, O God, is for ever and ever," Hebrews 1:8. And there is the same supreme respect and divine worship paid to him by the angels of heaven, as to God the Father, (verse 6.) "Let all the angels of God worship him."

But however he is thus above all, yet he is lowest of all in humility. There never was so great an instance of this virtue among either men or angels, as Jesus. None ever was so sensible of the distance between God and him, or had a heart so lowly before God, as the man Christ Jesus. Matthew 11:29. What a wonderful spirit of humility appeared in him, when he was here upon earth, in all his behaviour! In his contentment in his mean outward condition, contentedly living in the family of Joseph the carpenter, and Mary his mother, for thirty years together, and afterwards choosing outward meanness, poverty, and contempt, rather than earthly greatness; in his washing his disciples' feet, and in all his speeches and deportment towards them; in his cheerfully sustaining the form of a servant through his whole life, and submitting to such immense humiliation at death!

2. In the person of Christ do meet together infinite *majesty* and transcendent *meekness*. These again are two qualifications that meet together in no other person but Christ. Meekness, properly so called, is a virtue proper only to the creature: we scarcely ever find meekness mentioned as a divine attribute in Scripture; at least not in the New Testament; for thereby seems to be signified, a calmness and quietness of spirit, arising from humility in mutable beings that are naturally liable to be put into a ruffle by the assaults of a tempestuous and injurious world. But Christ being both God and man, hath both infinite majesty and superlative meekness.

Christ was a person of infinite majesty. It is he that is spoken of, Psalm 45:3. "Gird thy sword upon thy thigh, O most mighty, with thy glory and thy majesty." It is he that is mighty, that rideth on the heavens, and his excellency on the sky. It is he that is terrible out of his holy places; who is mightier than the noise of many waters, yea, than the mighty waves of the sea: before whom a fire goeth, and burneth up his enemies round about; at whose presence the earth quakes, and the hills melt; who sitteth on the circle of the earth, and all the inhabitants thereof are as grasshoppers; who rebukes the sea, and maketh it dry, and drieth up the rivers; whose eyes are as a flame of fire; from whose presence, and from the glory of whose power, the wicked shall be punished with everlasting destruction; who is the blessed and only Potentate, the King of kings, and Lord of lords, who hath heaven for his throne, and the earth for his footstool, and is the high and lofty One who inhabits eternity, whose kingdom is an everlasting kingdom, and of whose dominion there is no end.

And yet he was the most marvellous instance of meekness, and humble quietness of spirit, that ever was; agreeable to the *prophecies* of him, Matthew 21:4, 5. "All this was done, that it might be fulfilled which was spoken by the prophet, saying, Tell ye the daughter of Sion, Behold, thy King cometh unto thee, meek, and sitting upon an ass, and a colt the foal of an ass." And, agreeable to what Christ declares of himself, Matthew 11:29. "I am meek and lowly in heart." And agreeable to what was manifest in his behaviour: for there never was such an instance seen on earth, of a meek behaviour, under injuries and reproaches, and towards enemies; who, when he was reviled, reviled not again. He had a wonderful spirit of forgiveness, was ready to forgive his worst enemies, and prayed for them with fervent and effectual prayers. With what meekness did he appear in the ring of soldiers that were contemning and mocking him; he was silent, and opened not his mouth, but went as a lamb to the slaughter. Thus is Christ a Lion in majesty, and a Lamb in meekness.

3. There meet in the person of Christ the deepest *reverence* towards God and *equality* with God. Christ, when on earth, appeared full of holy reverence towards the Father. He paid the most reverential worship to him, praying to him with postures of reverence. Thus we read of his "kneeling down and praying," Luke 22:41. This became Christ, as one who had taken on him the human nature; but at the same time he existed in the divine nature; whereby his person was in all respects equal to the person of the Father. God the Father hath no attribute or perfection that the Son hath not, in equal degree, and equal glory. These things meet in no other person but Jesus Christ.

4. There are conjoined in the person of Christ

infinite *worthiness* of good, and the greatest *patience* under sufferings of evil. He was perfectly innocent, and deserved no suffering. He deserved nothing from God by any guilt of his own; and he deserved no ill from men. Yea, he was not only harmless and undeserving of suffering, but he was infinitely worthy; worthy of the infinite love of the Father, worthy of infinite and eternal happiness, and infinitely worthy of all possible esteem, love, and service from all men. And yet he was perfectly patient under the greatest sufferings that ever were endured in this world. Hebrews 12:2. "He endured the cross, despising the shame." He suffered not from his Father for his faults, but ours; and he suffered from men not for his faults, but for those things on account of which he was infinitely worthy of their love and honour; which made his patience the more wonderful and the more glorious. 1 Peter 2:20, etc. "For what glory is it, if when ye be buffeted for your faults, ye shall take it patiently, but if when ye do well, and suffer for it, ye take it patiently; this is acceptable with God. For even hereunto were ye called; because Christ also suffered for us, leaving us an example, that we should follow his steps: who did no sin, neither was guile found in his mouth: who when he was reviled, reviled not again; when he suffered, he threatened not; but committed himself to him that judgeth righteously: who his own self bare our sins in his own body on the tree, that we being dead to sin, should live unto righteousness: by whose stripes ye were healed." There is no such conjunction of innocence, worthiness, and patience under sufferings, as in the person of Christ.

5. In the person of Christ are conjoined an exceeding spirit of *obedience*, with supreme *dominion* over heaven and earth. Christ is the Lord of all things in two respects: he is so, as God-man and Mediator; and thus his dominion is appointed, and given him of the Father. Having it by delegation from God, he is as it were the Father's vicegerent. But he is Lord of all things in another respect, *viz.* as he is (by his original nature) God; and so he is by natural right the Lord of all, and supreme over all as much as the Father. Thus, he has dominion over the world, not by delegation, but in his own right. He is not an under God, as the Arians suppose, but, to all intents and purposes, supreme God.

And yet in the same person is found the greatest spirit of obedience to the commands and laws of God that ever was in the universe; which was manifest in his obedience here in this world. John 14:31. "As the Father gave me commandment, even so I do." John 15:10. "Even as I have kept my Father's commandments, and abide in his love." The greatness of his obedience appears in its perfection, and in his obeying commands of such exceeding difficulty. Never any one received commands from God of such difficulty, and that were so great a trial of obedience, as Jesus Christ. One of

God's commands to him was, that he should yield himself to those dreadful sufferings that he underwent. See John 10:18. "No man taketh it from me, but I lay it down of myself."—"This commandment received I of my Father." And Christ was thoroughly obedient to this command of God. Hebrews 5:8. "Though he were a Son, yet he learned obedience by the things that he suffered." Philippians 2:8. "He humbled himself, and became obedient unto death, even the death of the cross." Never was there such an instance of obedience in man or angel as this, though he was at the same time supreme Lord of both angels and men.

6. In the person of Christ are conjoined absolute *sovereignty* and perfect *resignation.* This is another unparalleled conjunction. Christ, as he is God, is the absolute sovereign of the world; the sovereign disposer of all events. The decrees of God are all his sovereign decrees; and the work of creation, and all God's works of providence, are his sovereign works. It is he that worketh all things according to the counsel of his own will. Colossians 1:16, 17. "By him, and through him, and to him, are all things." John 5:17. "The Father worketh hitherto, and I work." Matthew 8:3. "I will, be thou clean."

But yet Christ was the most wonderful instance of resignation that ever appeared in the world. He was absolutely and perfectly resigned when he had a near and immediate prospect of his terrible sufferings, and the dreadful cup that he was to drink. The idea and expectation of this made his soul exceeding sorrowful, even unto death, and put him into such an agony, that his sweat was as it were great drops or clots of blood, falling down to the ground. But in such circumstances he was wholly resigned to the will of God. Matthew 26:39. "O my Father, if it be possible, let this cup pass from me: nevertheless, not as I will, but as thou wilt." Verse 42. "O my Father, if this cup may not pass from me, except I drink it, thy will be done."

7. In Christ do meet together *self-sufficiency*, and an entire *trust* and reliance on God; which is another conjunction peculiar to the person of Christ. As he is a divine person, he is self-sufficient, standing in need of nothing. All creatures are dependent on him, but he is dependent on none, but is absolutely independent. His proceeding from the Father, in his eternal generation or filiation, argues no proper dependence on the *will* of the Father; for that proceeding was natural and *necessary*, and not arbitrary. But yet Christ entirely trusted in God: his enemies say that of him, "He trusted in God that he would deliver him," Matthew 27:43. And the apostle testifies, 1 Peter 2:23. "That he committed himself to God."

III. Such diverse excellencies are expressed in him towards men, that otherwise would have seemed impossible to be exercised towards the same object; as particularly these three, justice, mercy, and truth. The same that are mentioned Psalm 85:10. "Mercy and truth are met together, righteousness and peace have kissed each other." The strict justice of God, and even his revenging justice, and that against the sins of men, never was so gloriously manifested as in Christ. He manifested an infinite regard to the attribute of God's justice, in that, when he had a mind to save sinners, he was willing to undergo such extreme sufferings, rather than that their salvation should be to the injury of the honour of that attribute. And as he is the Judge of the world, he doth himself exercise strict justice; he will not clear the guilty, nor at all acquit the wicked in judgment. Yet how wonderfully is infinite mercy towards sinners displayed in him! And what glorious and ineffable grace and love have been and are exercised by him, towards sinful men! Though he be the just Judge of a sinful world, yet he is also the Saviour of the world. Though he be a consuming fire to sin, yet he is the light and life of sinners. Romans 3:25, 26, "Whom God hath set forth to be a propitiation, through faith in his blood, to declare his righteousness for the remission of sins that are past, through the forbearance of God; to declare, I say, at this time his righteousness, that he might be just, and the justifier of him which believeth in Jesus."

So the immutable truth of God, in the threatenings of his law against the sins of men, was never so manifested as it is in Jesus Christ; for there never was any other so great a trial of the unalterableness of the truth of God in those threatenings, as when sin came to be imputed to his own Son. And then in Christ has been seen already an actual complete accomplishment of those threatenings, which never has been nor will be seen in any other instance; because the eternity that will be taken up in fulfilling those threatenings on others, never will be finished. Christ manifested an infinite regard to this truth of God in his sufferings. And, in his judging the world, he makes the covenant of works, that contains those dreadful threatenings, his rule of judgment. He will see to it, that it is not infringed in the least jot or tittle: he will do nothing contrary to the threatenings of the law, and their complete fulfilment. And yet in him we have many great and precious promises, promises of perfect deliverance from the penalty of the law. And this is the promise that he hath promised us, even eternal life. And in him are all the promises of God, yea, and Amen.

Having thus shown wherein there is an admirable conjunction of excellencies in Jesus Christ, I now proceed,

Secondly, To show how this admirable conjunction of excellencies appears in Christ's *acts*.

I. It appears in what Christ did in taking on him our nature. In this act, his infinite condescension wonderfully appeared, that he who was God should become man; that the word should be made flesh, and should take on him a nature infinitely below his original nature! And it appears yet more remarkably in the low circumstances of his incarnation: he was conceived in the womb of a poor young woman, whose poverty appeared in this, when she came to offer sacrifices of her purification, she brought what was allowed of in the law only in case of poverty; as Luke 2:24. "According to what is said in the law of the Lord, a pair of turtle-doves, or two young pigeons." This was allowed only in case the person was so poor that she was not able to offer a lamb. Leviticus 12:8.

And though his infinite condescension thus appeared in the manner of his incarnation, yet his divine dignity also appeared in it; for though he was conceived in the womb of a poor virgin, yet he was conceived there by the power of the Holy Ghost. And his divine dignity also appeared in the holiness of his conception and birth. Though he was conceived in the womb of one of the corrupt race of mankind, yet he was conceived and born without sin; as the angel said to the blessed Virgin, Luke 1:35. "The Holy Ghost shall come upon thee, and the power of the Highest shall overshadow thee; therefore also that holy thing which shall be born of thee, shall be called the Son of God."

His infinite condescension marvellously appeared in the manner of his birth. He was brought forth in a stable, because there was no room for them in the inn. The inn was taken up by others, that were looked upon as persons of greater account. The blessed Virgin, being poor and despised, was turned or shut out. Though she was in such necessitous circumstances, yet those that counted themselves her betters would not give place to her; and therefore, in the time of her travail, she was forced to betake herself to a stable; and when the child was born, it was wrapped in swaddling-clothes, and laid in a manger. There Christ lay a little infant; and there he eminently appeared as a lamb. But yet this feeble infant, born thus in a stable, and laid in a manger, was born to conquer and triumph over Satan, that roaring lion. He came to subdue the mighty powers of darkness, and make a show of them openly; and so to restore peace on earth, and to manifest God's good-will towards men, and to bring glory to God in the highest; according as the end of his birth was declared by the joyful songs of the glorious hosts of angels appearing to the shepherds at the same time that the infant lay in the manger; whereby his divine dignity was manifested.

II. This admirable conjunction of excellencies appears in the acts and various passages of Christ's life. Though Christ dwelt in mean outward circumstances, whereby his condescension and humility especially appeared, and his majesty was veiled; yet his divine dignity and glory did in many of his acts shine through the veil, and it illustriously appeared, that he was not only the Son of man, but the great God.

Thus, in the circumstances of his infancy, his outward meanness appeared; yet there was something then to show forth his divine dignity, in the wise men's being stirred up to come from the east to give honour to him, their being led by a miraculous star, and coming and falling down and worshipping him, and presenting him with gold, frankincense, and myrrh. His humility and meekness wonderfully appeared in his subjection to his mother and reputed father when he was a child. Herein he appeared as a lamb. But his divine glory broke forth and shone when, at twelve years old, he disputed with doctors in the temple. In that he appeared, in some measure, as *the Lion of the tribe of Judah*.

And so, after he entered on his public ministry, his marvellous humility and meekness was manifested in his choosing to appear in such mean outward circumstances; and in being contented in them, when he was so poor that he had not where to lay his head, and depended on the charity of some of his followers for his subsistence; as appears by Luke 8, at the beginning. How meek, condescending, and familiar his treatment of his disciples; his discourses with them, treating them as a father his children; yea, as friends and companions. How patient, bearing such affliction and reproach, and so many injuries from the scribes and Pharisees, and others. In these things he appeared *as a Lamb*. And yet he at the same time did in many ways show forth his divine majesty and glory, particularly in the miracles he wrought, which were evidently divine works, and manifested omnipotent power, and so declared him to be *the Lion of the tribe of Judah*. His wonderful and miraculous works plainly showed him to be the God of nature; in that it appeared by them that he had all nature in his hands, and could lay an arrest upon it, and stop and change its course as he pleased. In healing the sick, and opening the eyes of the blind, and unstopping the ears of the deaf, and healing the lame; he showed that he was the God that framed the eye, and created the ear, and was the author of the frame of man's body. By the dead's rising at his command, it appeared that he was the author and fountain of life, and that "God the Lord, to whom belong the issues from death." By his walking on the sea in a storm, when the waves were raised, he showed himself to be that God spoken of in Job 9:8. "That treadeth on the waves of the sea." By his stilling the storm, and calming the rage of the sea, by his powerful command, saying, "Peace, be still," he showed that he has the command of the universe, and that he is that God who brings things to pass by the word of his power, who speaks and it is done, who commands and it stands fast; Psalm 65:7. "Who stilleth the noise of the seas, the noise of their waves." And Psalm 107:29. "That maketh the storm a calm, so that the waves thereof are still." And Psalm 89:8, 9. "O Lord God of hosts, who is a strong Lord like unto thee, or to thy faithfulness round about thee? Thou rulest the raging of the sea: when the waves thereof arise, thou stillest them." Christ, by casting out devils, remarkably appeared as *the Lion of the tribe of Judah*, and showed that he was stronger than the roaring lion, that seeks whom he may devour. He commanded them to come out, and they were forced to obey. They were terribly afraid of him; they fall down before him, and beseech him not to torment them. He forces a whole legion of them to forsake their hold, by his powerful word; and they could not so much as enter into the swine without his leave. He showed the glory of his omniscience, by telling the thoughts of men; as we have often an account. Herein he appeared to be that God spoken of, Amos 4:13. "That declareth unto man what is his thought." Thus, in the midst of his meanness and humiliation, his divine glory appeared in his miracles, John 2:11. "This beginning of miracles did Jesus in Cana of Galilee, and manifested forth his glory."

And though Christ ordinarily appeared without outward glory, and in great obscurity, yet at a certain time he threw off the veil, and appeared in his divine majesty, so far as it could be outwardly manifested to men in this frail state, when he was transfigured in the mount. The apostle Peter, 2 Peter 1:16, 17, was an "eye-witness of his majesty, when he received from God the Father honour and glory, when there came such a voice to him from the excellent glory, This is my beloved Son, in whom I am well pleased; which voice that came from heaven they heard, when they were with him in the holy mount." And at the same time that Christ was wont to appear in such meekness, condescension, and humility, in his familiar discourses with his disciples, appearing therein as the Lamb of God; he was also wont to appear as *The Lion of the tribe of Judah,* with divine authority and majesty, in his so sharply rebuking the scribes and Pharisees, and other hypocrites.

III. This admirable conjunction of excellencies remarkably appears in his offering up himself a sacrifice for sinners in his last sufferings. As this was the greatest thing in all the works of redemption, the greatest act of Christ in that work; so in this act especially does there appear that admirable conjunction of excellencies that has been spoken of. Christ never so much appeared as a lamb, as when he was slain: "He came like a lamb to the slaughter," Isaiah 53:7. Then he was offered up to God as a lamb without blemish, and without spot: then especially did he appear to be the anti-type of the lamb of the passover: 1 Corinthians 5:7, "Christ our Passover sacrificed for us." And yet in that act he did in an especial manner appear as *"the Lion of the tribe of Judah;"* yea, in this above all other acts, in many respects, as may appear in the following things.

1. Then was Christ in the greatest degree of his humiliation, and yet by that, above all other things, his divine glory appears. Christ's

humiliation was great, in being born in such a low condition, of a poor virgin, and in a stable. His humiliation was great, in being subject to Joseph the carpenter, and Mary his mother, and afterwards living in poverty, so as not to have where to lay his head; and in suffering such manifold and bitter reproaches as he suffered, while he went about preaching and working miracles. But his humiliation was never so great as it was in his last sufferings, beginning with his agony in the garden, till he expired on the cross. Never was he subject to such ignominy as then; never did he suffer so much pain in his body, or so much sorrow in his soul; never was he in so great an exercise of his condescension, humility, meekness, and patience, as he was in these last sufferings; never was his divine glory and majesty covered with so thick and dark a veil; never did he so empty himself and make himself of no reputation, as at this time. And yet, never was his divine glory so manifested, by any act of his, as in yielding himself up to these sufferings. When the fruit of it came to appear, and the mystery and ends of it to be unfolded in its issue, then did the glory of it appear; then did it appear as the most glorious act of Christ that ever he exercised towards the creature. This act of his is celebrated by the angels and hosts of heaven with peculiar praises, as that which is above all others glorious, as you may see in the context, ([Revelation 5] verse 9, etc.) "And they sung a new song, saying, Thou art worthy to take the book, and to open the seals thereof: for thou wast slain, and hast redeemed us to God by thy blood, out of every kindred, and tongue, and people, and nation; and hast made us unto our God kings and priests: and we shall reign on the earth. And I beheld, and I heard the voice of many angels round about the throne, and the beasts, and the elders: and the number of them was ten thousand times ten thousand, and thousands of thousands; saying with a loud voice, Worthy is the Lamb that was slain, to receive power, and riches, and wisdom, and strength, and honour, and glory, and blessing."

2. He never in any act gave so great a manifestation of love to God, and yet never so manifested his love to those that were enemies to God, as in that act. Christ never did any thing whereby his love to the Father was so eminently manifested, as in his laying down his life, under such inexpressible sufferings, in obedience to his command, and for the vindication of the honour of his authority and majesty; nor did ever any mere creature give such a testimony of love to God as that was. And yet this was the greatest expression of his love to sinful men who were enemies to God; Romans 5:10. "When we were enemies, we were reconciled to God, by the death of his Son." The greatness of Christ's love to such, appears in nothing so much as in its being dying love. That blood of Christ which fell in great drops to the ground, in

his agony, was shed from love to God's enemies, and his own. That shame and spitting, that torment of body, and that exceeding sorrow, even unto death, which he endured in his soul, was what he underwent from love to rebels against God, to save them from hell, and to purchase for them eternal glory. Never did Christ so eminently show his regard to God's honour, as in offering up himself a victim to justice. And yet in this above all, he manifested his love to them who dishonoured God, so as to bring such guilt on themselves, that nothing less than his blood could atone for it.

3. Christ never so eminently appeared *for* divine justice, and yet never suffered so much *from* divine justice, as when he offered up himself a sacrifice for our sins. In Christ's great sufferings, did his infinite regard to the honour of God's justice distinguishingly appear; for it was from regard to *that* that he thus humbled himself. And yet in these sufferings, Christ was the mark of the vindictive expressions of that very justice of God. Revenging justice then spent all its force upon him, on account of our guilt; which made him sweat blood, and cry out upon the cross, and probably rent his vitals—broke his heart, the fountain of blood, or some other blood vessels—and by the violent fermentation turned his blood to water. For the blood and water that issued out of his side, when pierced by the spear, seems to have been extravasated blood; and so there might be a kind of literal

fulfilment of Psalm 22:14. "I am poured out like water, and all my bones are out of joint: my heart is like wax, it is melted in the midst of my bowels." And this was the way and means by which Christ stood up for the honour of God's justice, *viz.* by thus suffering its terrible executions. For when he had undertaken for sinners, and had substituted himself in their room, divine justice could have its due honour no other way than by his suffering its revenges.—In this the diverse excellencies that met in the person of Christ appeared, *viz.* his infinite regard to God's justice, and such love to those that have exposed themselves to it, as induced him thus to yield himself a sacrifice to it.

4. Christ's holiness never so illustriously shone forth as it did in his last sufferings; and yet he never was to such a degree treated as guilty. Christ's holiness never had such a trial as it had then; and therefore never had so great a manifestation. When it was tried in this furnace, it came forth as gold, or as silver purified seven times. His holiness then above all appeared in his stedfast pursuit of the honour of God, and in his obedience to him. For his yielding himself unto death was transcendently the greatest act of obedience that ever was paid to God by any one since the foundation of the world.

And yet then Christ was in the greatest degree treated as a wicked person would have been. He was apprehended and bound as a malefactor. His accusers represented him as a most wicked wretch. In his sufferings before his crucifixion, he was treated as if he had been the worst and vilest of mankind; and then, he was put to a kind of death, that none but the worst sort of malefactors were wont to suffer, those that were most abject in their persons, and guilty of the blackest crimes. And he suffered as though guilty from God himself, by reason of our guilt imputed to him; for he who knew no sin, was made sin for us; he was made subject to wrath, as if he had been sinful himself. He was made a curse for us.

Christ never so greatly manifested his hatred of sin, as against God, as in his dying to take away the dishonour that sin had done to God; and yet never was he to such a degree subject to the terrible effects of God's hatred of sin, and wrath against it, as he was then. In this appears those diverse excellencies meeting in Christ, *viz.* love to God, and grace to sinners.

5. He never was so dealt with, as unworthy, as in his last sufferings; and yet it is chiefly on account of them that he is accounted worthy. He was therein dealt with as if he had not been worthy to live: they cry out, "Away with him! away with him! Crucify him." John 19:15. And they prefer Barabbas before him. And he suffered from the Father, as one whose demerits were infinite, by reason of our demerits that were laid upon him. And yet it was especially by that act of his subjecting himself to those sufferings, that he merited, and on the account of which

chiefly he was accounted worthy of the glory of his exaltation. Philippians 2:8, 9. "He humbled himself, and became obedient unto death; wherefore God hath highly exalted him." And we see that it is on this account chiefly, that he is extolled as worthy by saints and angels in the context; "Worthy," say they, "is the Lamb that was slain." This shows an admirable conjunction in him of infinite dignity, and infinite condescension and love to the infinitely unworthy.

6. Christ in his last sufferings suffered most extremely from those towards whom he was then manifesting his greatest act of love. He never suffered so much from his Father, (though not from any hatred to him, but from hatred to our sins,) for he then *forsook* him, or took away the comforts of his presence; and then "it pleased the Lord to bruise him, and put him to grief," as Isaiah 53:10. And yet never gave so great a manifestation of love to God as then, as has been already observed. So Christ never suffered so much from the hands of men as he did then; and yet never was in so high an exercise of love to men. He never was so ill treated by his disciples; who were so unconcerned about his sufferings, that they would not watch with him one hour, in his agony; and when he was apprehended, all forsook him and fled, except Peter, who denied him with oaths and curses. And yet then he was suffering, shedding his blood, and pouring out his soul unto death for them. Yea, he probably was then shedding his blood

for some of them that shed his blood; for whom he prayed while they were crucifying him; and who were probably afterwards brought home to Christ by Peter's preaching. (Compare Luke 23:34; Acts 2:23, 36, 37, 41; Acts 3:17, and Acts 4:4.) This shows an admirable meeting of justice and grace in the redemption of Christ.

7. It was in Christ's last sufferings, above all, that he was delivered up to the power of his enemies; and yet by these, above all, he obtained victory over his enemies. Christ never was so in his enemies' hands, as in the time of his last sufferings. They sought his life before; but from time to time they were restrained, and Christ escaped out of their hands; and this reason is given for it, that *his time was not yet come.* But now they were suffered to work their will upon him; he was in a great degree delivered up to the malice and cruelty of both wicked men and devils. And therefore when Christ's enemies came to apprehend him, he says to them, Luke 22:53. "When I was daily with you in the temple, ye stretched forth no hand against me: but this is your hour, and the power of darkness."

And yet it was principally by means of those sufferings that he conquered and overthrew his enemies. Christ never so effectually bruised Satan's head, as when Satan bruised his heel. The weapon with which Christ warred against the devil, and obtained a most complete victory and glorious triumph over him, was the cross, the instrument and weapon with which he thought he had overthrown Christ, and brought on him shameful destruction. Colossians 2:14, 15."Blotting out the handwriting of ordinances,—nailing it to his cross: and having spoiled principalities and powers, he made a show of them openly, triumphing over them in it." In his last sufferings, Christ sapped the very foundations of Satan's kingdom; he conquered his enemies in their own territories, and beat them with their own weapons; as David cut off Goliath's head with his own sword. The devil had, as it were, swallowed up Christ, as the whale did Jonah; but it was deadly poison to him; he gave him a mortal wound in his own bowels. He was soon sick of his morsel, and was forced to do by him as the whale did by Jonah. To this day he is heart-sick of what he then swallowed as his prey. In those sufferings of Christ was laid the foundation of all that glorious victory he has already obtained over Satan, in the overthrow of his heathenish kingdom in the Roman empire, and all the success the gospel has had since; and also of all his future and still more glorious victory that is to be obtained in the earth. Thus Samson's riddle is most eminently fulfilled, Judges 14:14. "Out of the eater came forth meat, and out of the strong came forth sweetness." And thus the true Samson does more towards the destruction of his enemies at his death than in his life; in yielding up himself to death, he pulls down the temple of Dagon, and destroys many thousands of his enemies, even while they are making themselves sport in his sufferings; and so he whose type was the ark, pulls down Dagon, and breaks off his head and hands in his own temple, even while he is brought in there as Dagon's captive.

Thus Christ appeared at the same time, and in the same act, as both a lion and a lamb. He appeared as a lamb in the hands of his cruel enemies; as a lamb in the paws, and between the devouring jaws, of a roaring lion; yea, he was a lamb actually slain by this lion: and yet at the same time, as *the Lion of the tribe of Judah*, he conquers and triumphs over Satan, destroying his own devourer; as Samson did the lion that roared upon him, when he rent him as he would a kid. And in nothing has Christ appeared so much as a lion, in glorious strength destroying his enemies, as when he was brought as a lamb to the slaughter. In his greatest weakness he was most strong; and when he suffered most from his enemies, he brought the greatest confusion on his enemies.—Thus this admirable conjunction of diverse excellencies was manifest in Christ, in his offering up himself to God in his last sufferings.

IV. It is still manifest in his acts, in his present state of exaltation in heaven. Indeed, in his exalted state, he most eminently appears in manifestation of those excellencies, on the account of which he is compared to a lion; but still he appears as a lamb; Revelation 14:1. "And I looked, and lo, a Lion stood on mount

Sion;" as in his state of humiliation he chiefly appeared as a lamb, and yet did not appear without manifestation of his divine majesty and power, as *the Lion of the tribe of Judah*. Though Christ be now at the right-hand of God, exalted as King of heaven, and Lord of the universe; yet as he still is in the human nature, he still excels in humility. Though the man Christ Jesus be the highest of all creatures in heaven, yet he as much excels them all in humility as he doth in glory and dignity; for none sees so much of the distance between God and him as he does. And though he now appears in such glorious majesty and dominion in heaven, yet he appears as a lamb in his condescending, mild, and sweet treatment of his saints there; for he is a Lamb still, even amidst the throne of his exaltation; and he that is the Shepherd of the whole flock is himself a Lamb, and goes before them in heaven as such. Revelation 7:17. "For the Lamb, which is in the midst of the throne, shall feed them, and shall lead them unto living fountains of waters, and God shall wipe away all tears from their eyes." Though in heaven every knee bows to him, and though the angels fall down before him adoring him, yet he treats his saints with infinite condescension, mildness, and endearment. And in his acts towards the saints on earth, he still appears as a lamb, manifesting exceeding love and tenderness in his intercession for them, as one that has had experience of affliction and temptation. He has not forgot what these things are; nor has he forgot how to pity those that are subject to them. And he still manifests his lamb-like excellencies, in his dealings with his saints on earth, in admirable forbearance, love, gentleness, and compassion. Behold him instructing, supplying, supporting, and comforting them; often coming to them, and manifesting himself to them by his Spirit, that he may sup with them, and they with him. Behold him admitting them to sweet communion, enabling them with boldness and confidence to come to him, and solacing their hearts. And in heaven Christ still appears, as it were, with the marks of his wounds upon him; and so appears as a Lamb as it had been slain; as he was represented in vision to St. John, in the text, when he appeared to open the book sealed with seven seals, which is part of the glory of his exaltation.

V. And *lastly*, this admirable conjunction of excellencies will be manifest in Christ's acts at the last judgment. He then, above all other times, will appear as *the Lion of the tribe of Judah* in infinite greatness and majesty, when he shall come in the glory of his Father, with all the holy angels, and the earth shall tremble before him, and the hills shall melt. This is he (Revelation 20:11.) "that shall sit on a great white throne, before whose face the earth and heaven shall flee away." He will then appear in the most dreadful and amazing manner to the wicked. The devils tremble at the thought of that appearance; and when it shall be, the kings, and the great men, and the rich men, and the chief captains, and the mighty men, and every bond-man, and every free-man, shall hide themselves in the dens, and in the rocks of the mountains, and shall cry to the mountains and rocks to fall on them, to hide them from the face and wrath of the Lamb. And none can declare or conceive of the amazing manifestations of wrath in which he will then appear towards these; or the trembling and astonishment, the shrieking and gnashing of teeth, with which they shall stand before his judgment-seat, and receive the terrible sentence of his wrath.

And yet he will at the same time appear as a Lamb to his saints; he will receive them as friends and brethren, treating them with infinite mildness and love. There shall be nothing in him terrible to them; but towards them he will clothe himself wholly with sweetness and endearment. The church shall be then admitted to him as his bride; that shall be her wedding-day. The saints shall all be sweetly invited to come with him to inherit the kingdom, and reign in it with him to all eternity.

APPLICATION

I. From this doctrine we may learn one reason why Christ is called by such a variety of names, and held forth under such a variety of representations, in Scripture. It is the better to signify and exhibit to us that variety of excellencies that meet together and are conjoined in him. Many appellations are mentioned together in one verse, Isaiah 9:6. "For unto us a Child is born, unto us a Son is given, and the government shall be upon his shoulder: and his name shall be called Wonderful, Counsellor, the mighty God, the everlasting Father, the Prince of Peace." It shows a wonderful conjunction of excellencies, that the same person should be a Son, born and given, and yet be the everlasting Father, without beginning or end; that he should be a Child, and yet be he whose name is Counsellor, and the mighty God; and well may his name, in whom such things are conjoined, be called Wonderful.

By reason of the same wonderful conjunction, Christ is represented by a great variety of sensible things, that are on some account excellent. Thus in some places he is called a Sun, as Malachi 4:2, in others a Star, Numbers 24:17. And he is especially represented by the Morning-star, as being that which excels all other stars in brightness, and is the forerunner of the day, Revelation 22:16. And, as in our text, he is compared to a lion in one verse, and a lamb in the next, so sometimes he is compared to a roe or a young hart, another creature most diverse from a lion. So in some places he is called a rock, in others he is compared to a pearl. In some places he is called a man of war, and the Captain of our Salvation, in other places he is represented as a bridegroom. In the second chapter of Canticles, the 1st verse, he is compared to a rose and lily, that are sweet and beautiful flowers; in the next verse but one, he is compared to a tree bearing sweet fruit. In Isaiah 53:2, he is called a Root out of a dry ground; but elsewhere, instead of that, he is called the Tree of Life, that grows (not in a dry or barren ground, but) "in the midst of the paradise of God," Revelation 2:7.

II. Let the consideration of this wonderful meeting of diverse excellencies in Christ induce you to accept of him, and close with him as your Saviour. As all manner of excellencies meet in him, so there are concurring in him all manner of arguments and motives, to move you to choose him for your Saviour, and every thing that tends to encourage poor sinners to come and put their trust in him: his fullness and all-sufficiency as a Saviour gloriously appear in that variety of excellencies that has been spoken of.

Fallen man is in a state of exceeding great misery, and is helpless in it; he is a poor weak creature, like an infant cast out in its blood in the day that it is born. But Christ is *the Lion of the tribe of Judah;* he is strong, though we are weak; he hath prevailed to do that for us which no creature else could do. Fallen man is a mean despicable creature, a contemptible worm; but Christ, who has undertaken for us, is infinitely honourable and worthy. Fallen man is polluted, but Christ is infinitely holy; fallen man is hateful, but Christ is infinitely lovely; fallen man is the object of God's indignation, but Christ is infinitely dear to him. We have dreadfully provoked God, but Christ has performed that righteousness which is infinitely precious in God's eyes.

And here is not only infinite strength and infinite worthiness, but infinite condescension, and love and mercy, as great as power and dignity. If you are a poor, distressed sinner, whose heart is ready to sink for fear that God never will have mercy on you, you need not be afraid to go to Christ, for fear that he is either unable or unwilling to help you. Here is a strong foundation, and an inexhaustible treasure, to answer the necessities of your poor soul; and here is infinite grace and gentleness to invite and imbolden a poor, unworthy, fearful soul to come to it. If Christ accepts of you, you need not fear but that you will be safe; for he is a strong Lion for your defence. And if you come, you need not fear but that you shall be accepted; for he is like a Lamb to all that come to him, and receives them with infinite grace and tenderness. It is true he has awful majesty; he is the great God, and infinitely high above you; but there is this to encourage and imbolden the poor sinner, that Christ is man as well as God; he is a creature, as well as the Creator; and he is the most humble and lowly in heart of any creature in heaven or earth. This may well make the poor unworthy creature bold in coming to him. You need not hesitate one moment; but may run to him, and cast yourself upon him. You will certainly be graciously and meekly received by him. Though he is a lion, he will only be a lion to your enemies; but he will be a lamb to you. It could not have been conceived, had it not been so in the person of Christ, that there could have been so much in any Saviour, that is inviting and tending to encourage sinners to trust in him. Whatever your circumstances are, you need not be afraid to come to such a Saviour as this. Be you never so wicked a creature, here is worthiness enough; be you never so poor, and mean, and ignorant a creature, there is no danger of being despised; for though he be so much greater than you, he is also immensely more humble than you. Any one of you that is a father or mother, will not despise one of your own children that comes to you in distress: much less danger is there of Christ despising you, if you in your heart come to him. Here let me a little expostulate with the poor, burdened, distressed soul.

1. What are you afraid of, that you dare not venture your soul upon Christ? Are you afraid that he cannot save you; that he is not strong enough to conquer the enemies of your soul? But how can you desire one stronger than the "mighty God?" as Christ is called, Isaiah 9:6. Is there need of greater than infinite strength? Are you afraid that he will not be willing to stoop so low as to take any gracious notice of you? But then, look on him, as he stood in the ring of soldiers, exposing his blessed face to be buffeted and spit upon by them! Behold him bound with

his back uncovered to those that smote him! And behold him hanging on the cross! Do you think that he that had condescension enough to stoop to these things, and that for his crucifiers, will be unwilling to accept of you if you come to him? Or, are you afraid that if he does accept of you, that God the Father will not accept of him for you? But consider, will God reject his own Son, in whom his infinite delight is, and has been, from all eternity, and who is so united to him, that if he should reject him he would reject himself?

2. What is there that you can desire should be in a Saviour, that is not in Christ? Or, wherein should you desire a Saviour should be otherwise than Christ is? What excellency is there wanting? What is there that is great or good; what is there that is venerable or winning; what is there that is adorable or endearing; or, what can you think of that would be encouraging, which is not to be found in the person of Christ? Would you have your Saviour to be great and honourable, because you are not willing to be beholden to a mean person? And, is not Christ a person honourable enough to be worthy that you should be dependent on him; is he not a person high enough to be appointed to so honourable a work as your salvation? Would you not only have a Saviour of high degree, but would you have him, notwithstanding his exaltation and dignity, to be made also of low degree, that he might have experience of afflictions and trials, that he might learn

by the things that he has suffered, to pity them that suffer and are tempted? And has not Christ been made low enough for you? and has he not suffered enough? Would you not only have him possess experience of the afflictions you now suffer, but also of that amazing wrath that you fear hereafter, that he may know how to pity those that are in danger, and afraid of it? This Christ has had experience of, which experience gave him a greater sense of it, a thousand times, than you have, or any man living has. Would you have your Saviour to be one who is near to God, that so his mediation might be prevalent with him? And can you desire him to be nearer to God than Christ is, who is his only-begotten Son, of the same essence with the Father? And would you not only have him near to God, but also near to you, that you may have free access to him? And would you have him nearer to you than to be in the same nature, united to you by a spiritual union, so close as to be fitly represented by the union of the wife to the husband, of the branch to the vine, of the member to the head; yea, so as to be one spirit? For so he will be united to you, if you accept of him. Would you have a Saviour that has given some great and extraordinary testimony of mercy and love to sinners, by something that he has done, as well as by what he says? And can you think or conceive of greater things than Christ has done? Was it not a great thing for him, who was God, to take upon him human nature; to be not only

God, but man thenceforward to all eternity? But would you look upon suffering for sinners to be a yet greater testimony of love to sinners, than merely doing, though it be ever so extraordinary a thing that he has done? And would you desire that a Saviour should suffer more than Christ has suffered for sinners? What is there wanting, or what would you add if you could, to make him more fit to be your Saviour? But further, to induce you to accept of Christ as your Saviour, consider two things particularly.

(1.) How much Christ appears as the Lamb of God in his invitations to you to come to him and trust in him. With what sweet grace and kindness does he, from time to time, call and invite you; as Proverbs 8:4. "Unto you, O men, I call, and my voice is to the sons of men." And Isaiah 55:1, 2, 3. "Ho, every one that thirsteth, come ye to the waters, and he that hath no money; come ye, buy and eat; yea, come, buy wine and milk without money, and without price." How gracious is he here in inviting every one that thirsts, and in so repeating his invitation over and over, "Come ye to the waters; come, buy and eat; yea, come!" Mark the excellency of that entertainment which he invites you to accept of, "Come, buy wine and milk!" your poverty, having nothing to pay for it, shall be no objection,— "Come, he that hath no money, come without money, and without price!" What gracious arguments and expostulations he uses with you! "Wherefore do ye spend money for that which is not bread? and your labour for that which satisfieth not? Hearken diligently unto me, and eat ye that which is good, and let your soul delight itself in fatness." As much as to say, It is altogether needless for you to continue labouring and toiling for that which can never serve your turn, seeking rest in the world, and in your own righteousness:—I have made abundant provision for you, of that which is really good, and will fully satisfy your desires, and answer your end, and stand ready to accept of you: you need not be afraid; if you will come to me, I will engage to see all your wants supplied, and you made a happy creature. As he promises in the third verse, "Incline your ear, and come unto me: Hear, and your soul shall live, and I will make an everlasting covenant with you, even the sure mercies of David." And so, Proverbs 9 at the beginning. How gracious and sweet is the invitation there! "Whoso is simple, let him turn in hither;" let you be never so poor, ignorant, and blind a creature, you shall be welcome. And in the following words, Christ sets forth the provision that he has made for you, "Come, eat of my bread, and drink of the wine which I have mingled." You are in a poor famishing state, and have nothing wherewith to feed your perishing soul; you have been seeking something, but yet remain destitute. Hearken, how Christ calls you to eat of his bread, and to drink of the wine that he hath mingled! And how much like a lamb does Christ appear in Matthew 11:28–30. "Come unto me, all ye that labour and are heavy laden, and I will give you rest. Take my yoke upon you, and learn of me, for I am meek and lowly in heart; and ye shall find rest to your souls. For my yoke is easy, and my burden is light." O thou poor distressed soul! whoever thou art, consider that Christ mentions thy very case, when he calls to them who labour and are heavy laden! How he repeatedly promises you rest if you come to him! In the 28th verse he says, "I will give you rest." And in the 29th verse, "Ye shall find rest to your souls." This is what you want. This is the thing you have been so long in vain seeking after. O how sweet would rest be to you, if you could but obtain it! Come to Christ, and you shall obtain it. And hear how Christ, to encourage you, represents himself as a lamb! He tells you, that he is meek and lowly in heart; and are you afraid to come to such a one? And again, Revelation 3:20. "Behold, I stand at the door and knock: if any man hear my voice, and open the door, I will come in to him, and I will sup with him, and he with me." Christ condescends not only to call you to him, but he comes to you; he comes to your door, and there knocks. He might send an officer and seize you as a rebel and vile malefactor; but instead of that, he comes and knocks at your door, and seeks that you would receive him into your house, as your Friend and Saviour. And he not only knocks at your door, but he stands there waiting, while you are backward and unwilling. And not only so, but he makes promises what he will do for you, if you will admit him, what privileges he will admit you to; he will sup with you, and you with him. And again, Revelation 22:16, 17. "I am the root and the offspring of David, and the bright and morning star. And the Spirit and the bride say, Come. And let him that heareth, say, come. And let him that is athirst come. And whosoever will, let him take of the water of life freely." How does Christ here graciously set before you his own winning attractive excellency! And how does he condescend to declare to you not only his own invitation, but the invitation of the Spirit and the bride, if by any means he might encourage you to come! And how does he invite every one that will, that they may "take of the water of life freely," that they may take it as a free gift, however precious it be, and though it be the water of life!

(2.) If you do come to Christ, he will appear as a Lion, in his glorious power and dominion, to defend you. All those excellencies of his, in which he appears as a lion, shall be yours, and shall be employed for you in your defence, for your safety, and to promote your glory; he will be as a lion to fight against your enemies. He that touches you, or offends you, will provoke his wrath, as he that stirs up a lion. Unless your enemies can conquer this Lion, they shall not be able to destroy or hurt you; unless they are stronger than he, they shall not be able to hinder your happiness. Isaiah 31:4. "For thus hath the Lord spoken unto me, Like as the lion and the young lion roaring on his prey, when a multitude of shepherds is called forth against him, he will not be afraid of their voice, nor abase himself for the noise of them; so shall the Lord of hosts come down to fight for mount Zion, and for the hill thereof."

III. Let what has been said be improved to induce you to love the Lord Jesus Christ, and choose him for your friend and portion. As there is such an admirable meeting of diverse excellencies in Christ, so there is every thing in him to render him worthy of your love and choice, and to win and engage it. Whatsoever there is or can be desirable in a friend, is in Christ, and that to the highest degree that can be desired.

Would you choose for a friend a person of great dignity? It is a thing taking with men to have those for their friends who are much above them; because they look upon themselves honoured by the friendship of such. Thus, how taking would it be with an inferior maid to be the object of the dear love of some great and excellent prince. But Christ is infinitely above you, and above all the princes of the earth; for he is the King of kings. So honourable a person as this offers himself to you, in the nearest and dearest friendship.

And would you choose to have a friend not only great but good? In Christ infinite greatness and infinite goodness meet together, and receive lustre and glory one from another. His greatness is rendered lovely by his goodness. The greater any one is without goodness, so much the greater evil; but when infinite goodness is joined with greatness, it renders it a glorious and adorable greatness. So, on the other hand, his infinite goodness receives lustre from his greatness. He that is of great understanding and ability, and is withal of a good and excellent disposition, is deservedly more esteemed than a lower and lesser being, with the same kind inclination and good will. Indeed goodness is excellent in whatever subject it be found; it is beauty and excellency itself, and renders all excellent that are possessed of it; and yet most excellent when joined with greatness. The very same excellent qualities of gold render the body in which they are inherent more precious, and of greater value, when joined with greater than when with lesser dimensions. And how glorious is the sight, to see him who is the great Creator and supreme Lord of heaven and earth, full of condescension, tender pity and mercy, towards the mean and unworthy! His almighty power, and infinite majesty and self-sufficiency, render his exceeding love and grace the more surprising. And how do his condescension and compassion endear his majesty, power, and dominion, and render those attributes pleasant, that would otherwise be only terrible! Would you not desire that your friend, though great and honourable, should be of such condescension and grace, and so to have the way opened to free access to him, that his exaltation above you might not hinder your free enjoyment of his friendship?—And would you choose not only that the infinite greatness and majesty of your friend should be, as it were, mollified and sweetened with condescension and grace; but would you also desire to have your friend brought nearer to you? Would you choose a friend far above you, and yet as it were upon a level with you too? Though it be taking with men to have a near and dear friend of superior dignity, yet there is also an inclination in them to have their friend a sharer with them in circumstances. Thus is Christ. Though he be the great God, yet he has, as it were, brought himself down to be upon a level with you, so as to become man as you are, that he might not only be your Lord, but your brother, and that he might be the more fit to be a companion for such a worm of the dust. This is one end of Christ's taking upon him man's nature, that his people might be under advantages for a more familiar converse with him, than the infinite distance of the divine nature would allow of. And upon this account the church longed for Christ's incarnation, Song of Solomon 8:1. "O that thou wert my brother, that sucked the breasts of my mother! when I should find thee without, I would kiss thee, yea, I should not be despised." One design of God in the gospel, is to bring us to make God the object of our undivided respect, that he may engross our regard every way, that whatever natural inclination there is in our souls, he may be the centre of it; that God may be all in all. But there is an inclination in the creature, not only to the adoration of a Lord and Sovereign, but to complacence in some one as a friend, to love and delight in some one that may be conversed with as a companion. And virtue and holiness do not destroy or weaken this inclination of our nature. But so hath God contrived in the affair of our redemption, that a divine person may be the object even of this inclination of our nature. And in order hereto, such an one is come down to us; and has taken our nature, and is become one of us, and calls himself our friend, brother, and companion. Psalm 122:8. "For my brethren and companions' sake, will I now say, Peace be within thee."

But is it not enough in order to invite and encourage you to free access to a friend so great and high, that he is one of infinite condescending grace, and also has taken your own nature, and is become man? But would you, further to imbolden and win you, have him a man of wonderful meekness and humility? Why, such an one is Christ! He is not only become man for you, but far the meekest and most humble of all men, the greatest instance of these sweet virtues that ever was, or will be. And besides these, he has all other human excellencies in the highest perfection. These, indeed, are no proper addition to his divine excellencies. Christ has no more excellency in his person, since his incarnation, than he had before; for divine excellency is infinite, and cannot be added to. Yet his human excellencies are additional *manifestations* of his glory and excellency to us, and are additional recommendations of him to our esteem and love, who are of finite comprehension. Though his human excellencies are but communications and reflections of his divine; and though this light, as reflected, falls infinitely short of the divine fountain of light in its immediate glory; yet the reflection shines not without its proper advantages, as presented to our view and affection. The glory of Christ in the qualifications of his human nature, appears to us in excellencies that are of our own kind, and are exercised in our own way and manner; and so, in some respects, are peculiarly fitted to invite our acquaintance and draw our affection. The glory of Christ as it appears in his divinity, though far brighter, more dazzles our eyes, and exceeds the strength of our sight or our comprehension; but, as it shines in the human excellencies of Christ, it is brought more to a level with our conceptions, and suitableness to our nature and manner, yet retaining a semblance of the same divine beauty, and a savour of the same divine sweetness. But as both divine and human excellencies meet together in Christ, they set off and recommend each other to us. It tends to endear the divine majesty and holiness of Christ to us, that these are attributes of one in our nature, one of us, who is become our brother, and is the meekest and humblest of men. It encourages us to look upon these divine perfections, however high and great; since we have some near concern in, and liberty freely to enjoy them. And on the other hand, how much more glorious and surprising do the meekness, the humility, obedience, resignation, and other human excellencies of Christ appear, when we consider that they are in so great a person, as the eternal Son of God, the Lord of heaven and earth!

By your choosing Christ for your friend and portion, you will obtain these two infinite benefits.

1. Christ will give himself to you, with all those various excellencies that meet in him, to your full and everlasting enjoyment. He will ever after treat you as his dear friend; and you shall ere long be where he is, and shall behold his glory, and dwell with him, in most free and intimate communion and enjoyment.

When the saints get to heaven, they shall not merely see Christ, and have to do with him as subjects and servants with a glorious and gracious Lord and Sovereign, but Christ will entertain them as friends and brethren. This we may learn from the manner of Christ's conversing with his disciples here on earth: though he was their sovereign Lord, and did not refuse, but required, their supreme respect and adoration, yet he did not treat them as earthly sovereigns are wont to do their subjects. He did not keep them at an awful distance; but all along conversed with them with the most friendly familiarity, as a father amongst a company of children, yea, as with brethren. So he did with the twelve, and so he did with Mary, Martha, and Lazarus. He told his disciples, that he did not call them servants, but friends; and we read of one of them that leaned on his bosom: and doubtless he will not treat his disciples with less freedom and endearment in heaven. He will not keep them at a greater distance for his being in a state of exaltation; but he will rather take them into a state of exaltation with him. This will be the improvement Christ will make of his own glory, to make his beloved friends partakers with him, to glorify them in his glory, as he says to his Father, John 17:22, 23. "And the glory which thou hast given me, have I given them, that they may be one, even as we are one; I in them," etc. We are to consider, that though Christ is greatly exalted, yet he is exalted, not as a private person for himself only, but as his people's head; he is exalted in their name, and upon their account, as the first fruits, and as representing the whole harvest. He is not exalted that he may be at a greater distance from them, but that they may be exalted with him. The exaltation and honour of the head is not to make a greater distance between the head and the members; but the members have the same relation and union with the head they had before, and are honoured with the head; and instead of the distance being greater, the union shall be nearer and more perfect. When believers get to heaven, Christ will conform them to himself; as he is set down in his Father's throne, so they shall sit down with him on his throne, and shall in their measure be made like him.

When Christ was going to heaven, he comforted his disciples with the thought, that after a while, he would come again and take them to himself, that they might be with him. And we are not to suppose that when the disciples got to heaven, they found him keeping a greater distance than he used to do. No, doubtless, he embraced them as friends, and welcomed them to his and their Father's house, and to his and their glory. They who had been his friends in this world, who had been together with him here, and had together partaken of sorrows and troubles, are now welcomed by him to rest, and to partake of glory with him. He took them and led them into his chambers, and showed them all his glory; as he prayed, John 17:24. "Father, I will that they also whom thou hast given me, be with me, that they may behold the glory which thou hast given me." And he led them to his living fountains of waters, and made them partake of his delights; as he prays, John 17:13. "That my joy may be fulfilled in themselves;" and set them down with him at his table in his kingdom, and made them partake with him of his dainties, according to his promise, Luke 22:30, and led them into his banqueting house, and made them to drink new wine with him in the kingdom of his heavenly Father, as he foretold them when he instituted the Lord's supper, Matt. 26:29.

Yea, the saints' conversation with Christ in heaven shall not only be as intimate, and their access to him as free, as of the disciples on earth, but in many respects much more so; for in heaven, that vital union shall be perfect, which is exceeding imperfect here. While the saints are in this world, there are great remains of sin and darkness, to separate or disunite them from Christ, which shall then all be removed. This is not a time for that full acquaintance, and those glorious manifestations of love, which Christ designs for his people hereafter; which seems to be signified by his speech to Mary Magdalene, when ready to embrace him, when she met him after his resurrection; John 20:17. "Jesus saith unto her, Touch me not; for I am not yet ascended to my Father."

When the saints shall see Christ's glory and exaltation in heaven, it will indeed possess their hearts with the greater admiration and adoring respect, but will not awe them into any separation, but will serve only to heighten their surprise and joy, when they find Christ condescending to admit them to such intimate access, and so freely and fully communicating himself to them. So that if we choose Christ for our friend and portion, we shall hereafter be so received to him, that there shall be nothing to hinder the fullest enjoyment of him, to the satisfying the utmost cravings of our souls. We may take our full swing at gratifying our spiritual appetite after these holy pleasures. Christ will then say, as in Song of Solomon 5:1. "Eat, O friends, drink, yea, drink abundantly, O beloved." And this shall be our entertainment to all eternity! There shall never be any end of this happiness, or any thing to interrupt our enjoyment of it, or in the least to molest us in it!

2. By your being united to Christ, you will have a more glorious union with and enjoyment of God the Father, than otherwise could be. For hereby the saints' relation to God becomes much nearer; they are the children of God in a higher manner than otherwise could be. For, being members of God's own Son, they are in a sort partakers of his relation to the Father: they are not only sons of God by regeneration, but by a kind of communion in the sonship of the eternal Son. This seems to be intended, Galatians 4:4, 5, 6. "God sent forth his Son, made of a woman, made under the law, to redeem them that are under the law, that we might receive the adoption of sons. And because ye are sons, God hath sent forth the Spirit of his Son into your hearts, crying, Abba, Father." The church is the daughter of God, not only as he hath begotten her by his word and Spirit, but as she is the spouse of his eternal Son.

So we being members of the Son, are partakers in our measure of the Father's love to the Son, and complacence in him. John 17:23. "I in them, and thou in me,—Thou hast loved them as thou hast loved me." And verse 26, "That the love wherewith thou hast loved me may be in them." And John 16:27. "The Father himself loveth you, because ye have loved me, and have believed that I came out from God." So we shall, according to our capacities, be partakers of the Son's enjoyment of God, and have his joy fulfilled in ourselves, John 17:13. And by this means we shall come to an immensely higher, more intimate and full enjoyment of God, than otherwise could have been. For there is doubtless an infinite intimacy between the Father and the Son; which is expressed by his being in the bosom of the Father. And saints being in him, shall, in their measure and manner, partake with him in it, and of the blessedness of it.

And thus is the affair of our redemption ordered, that thereby we are brought to an immensely more exalted kind of union with God, and enjoyment of him, both the Father and the Son, than otherwise could have been. For Christ being united to the human nature, we have advantage for a more free and full enjoyment of him, than we could have had if he had remained only in the divine nature. So again, we being united to a divine person, as his members, can have a more intimate union and intercourse with God the Father, who is only in the divine nature, than otherwise could be. Christ, who is a divine person, by taking on him our nature, descends from the infinite distance and height above us, and is brought nigh to us; whereby we have advantage for the full enjoyment of him. And, on the other hand, we, by being in Christ a divine person, do as it were ascend up to God, through the infinite distance, and have hereby advantage for the full enjoyment of him also.

This was the design of Christ, that he, and his Father, and his people, might all be united in one. John 17:21–23. "That they all may be one, as thou, Father, art in me, and I in thee; that they also may be one in us; that the world may believe that thou hast sent me. And the glory which thou hast given me, I have given them, that they may be one, even as we are one; I in them and thou in me, that they may be made perfect in one." Christ has brought it to pass, that those whom the Father has given him should be brought into the household of God; that he and his Father, and his people, should be as one society, one family; that the church should be as it were admitted into the society of the blessed Trinity.

NOTES

NOTES

MAN'S QUESTIONS & GOD'S ANSWERS

Am I accountable to God?
"Every one of us shall give account of himself to God." (Romans 14:12).

Has God seen all my ways?
"All things are naked and opened unto the eyes of Him with whom we have to do." (Hebrews 4:13).

Does He charge me with sin?
"The Scripture hath concluded all under sin." (Galatians 3:22).
"All have sinned." (Romans 3:23).

Will He punish sin?
"The soul that sinneth, it shall die." (Ezekiel 18:4).
"For the wages of sin is death." (Romans 6:23).

Must I perish?
"God is not willing that any perish, but that all should come to repentance." (2 Peter 3:9).

How can I escape?
"Believe on the Lord Jesus Christ, and thou shalt be saved." (Acts 16:31).

Is He able to save me?
"He is able also to save them to the uttermost that come unto God by Him." (Hebrews 7:25).

Is He willing?
"Christ Jesus came into the world to save sinners." (1 Timothy 1:15).

Am I saved on believing?
"He that believeth on the Son hath everlasting life." (John 3:36).

Can I be saved now?
"Now is the accepted time; behold, now is the day of salvation." (2 Corinthians 6:2).

As I am?
"Him that cometh to Me I will in no wise cast out." (John 6:37).

Shall I not fall away?
"Him that is able to keep you from falling." (Jude 24).

If saved, how should I live?

"They which live should not henceforth live unto themselves, but unto Him which died for them." (2 Corinthians 5:15).

What about death, and eternity?
"I go to prepare a place for you; that where I am, there ye may be also." (John 14:2, 3).

Made in the USA
Lexington, KY
23 April 2016